Creating Leaders and Organizations of Greatness

A How-To Guide

Greg Selker

ISBN: 0986406805
ISBN-13: 978-0986406805

TO MY TEACHERS

.

CONTENTS

ACKNOWLEDGMENTS

To the executives I have interviewed over my career who have been my teachers. To my numerous clients who graciously invite me into their organizations and their lives. To my co-worker Martha whose dedication, insights and coaching always make me a better consultant, leader and person.

To my friends — Thomas who encouraged me to write this book, and Larry for his ongoing support.

To my editors — Aileen Cho who helped me construct better and simpler sentences, and my father Eugene who helped me simplify and clarify my thoughts.

To my father and the memory of my grandfather. The two individuals who first clearly distinguished and demonstrated ethical conduct to me that cut across their businesses, friends and family.

To my wife Lois for her ongoing love and support. She continually chooses me to be "the one" for her and in her life, and I am eternally grateful for that.

I thank you all for the gift of your many contributions.

1. THE CONSPIRACY OF AVERAGE

There is an unwritten and unspoken conspiracy in which a majority of the world's companies and organizations, their leaders, boards and employees participate. It is a conspiracy to maintain an unwitting standard — a status quo of mediocrity across their culture, their actions and results.

Yes, there are exceptions. There are companies and organizations that achieve financial success for a sustained period of time. A select number of these even find a way to move from sustained financial success into actually achieving and delivering greatness. But these are rare instances indeed. If we're generous, they can be counted on two hands.

The vast majority of companies that find a pathway for sustained financial success eventually succumb to a predictable leveling off of growth. This is generally accompanied by a decline in innovation, by lower valuation in the public marketplace, by cultures that become stagnant and are less vibrant, by a diminishing quality of talent and leadership that is hired and developed, and by a lower quality of goods and services that are in turn delivered to a shrinking customer base.

In other words, mediocrity begins to hold sway over these companies and organizations like a virus that you can't get rid of, and over time your diminished capabilities become your new "normal" state of being.

Even if a company is successful in growing its revenue, even if a company has something that the marketplace wants and needs, the specter of mediocrity eventually creeps its way into the culture of the organization — infecting its processes and infrastructure and dampening the capabilities of its leaders and workforce.

It is almost as if an epidemic has infected all companies and organizations regardless of country of origin, size and language spoken day-to-day in the hallways and offices. Whether it is a company designed for maximum profit, or an organization committed to the most altruistic goals possible, the conspiracy to produce and maintain "average" ultimately holds sway.

This unwritten and unspoken conspiracy exists in spite of what is taught and learned in the best business schools to our current and future leaders. The staffing and deployment of millions of average leaders and employees continues to occur, regardless of the latest ideas of human resources professionals and human resources information systems. These organizations continue to turn out average leaders who manage average employees within average environments. This is so notwithstanding the money and time spent on leadership development, which decreased significantly after the global economic downturn of 2008 and is now starting to slightly grow again.

No matter how altruistic or compelling the purpose of a non-profit organization, it is often for naught. The organization may be committed to what would universally be described as a world- and life-changing mission. However, as soon as that organization begins to achieve success, grow and hire more and more people, it is most likely taking steps down the path of near-certain mediocrity and average results.

The Conspiracy of Average is unknowingly sustained by both major and supporting players.

The supporting players include business schools geared both toward for-profit and non-profit organizations, industrial psychologists and organizational development consultants, and boards of directors who provide oversight on a part-time basis. Other ancillary minor players and unwitting supporters of the conspiracy are various professional organizations and societies that focus on specific functional areas of expertise.

The major players in the conspiracy are found in the three separate categories of leadership, human resources and staffing. These are represented by:

- CEOs and their functional and business leaders who in turn are running and managing their own organizations;
- Chief Human Resources Officers (CHROs) and their supporting HR organizations;
- Staffing encompassing both internal recruiting, and external recruiters/search firms at both the executive and lower levels

These three major categories, for the sake of simplicity let's call them leaders, HR and recruiters, act as the legs of a three-legged stool that sustains the global conspiracy for mediocrity.

The rare examples of sustained success, and even the rarer examples of greatness, point to the possibility that this conspiracy for mediocrity does not need to hold sway. Over my career as an executive search and leadership consultant, I have spent thousands of hours interviewing and assessing executives to discover whether there are best practices that can be identified and implemented to move an individual and organization reliably toward greatness.

This book is the result of this 26-year-long inquiry into understanding the conditions that keep the Conspiracy of Average in place and identifying possible ways of moving oneself and one's organization beyond it. I have discovered some simple practices for both individuals and organizations that, if practiced and implemented on a repeatable basis, reliably deal a death blow to the conditions that enforce a state of mediocrity and average. These practices lay a firm foundation to create both Leaders and Organizations of Greatness.

But before we get to the solution, we need to better understand the problem. We need to fully expose the conditions that keep the Conspiracy of Average in place and understand the impact this has on our three major players.

Welcome to my journey down the rabbit hole!

2. PAY NO ATTENTION TO THE MAN BEHIND THE CURTAIN

The Conspiracy of Average is a result of us waking up every morning and moving into our lives thinking what we think, speaking the words we say, making the decisions we make and taking the actions that produce our results. In other words, the conspiracy unwittingly arises from the very fabric of how we live our lives and interact with those around us.

Just like in *The Wizard of Oz*, something is going on right in front of us but the overriding message we hear is, "Pay no attention to the

Conspiracy of Average and what keeps it in place."

This does not mean that we consciously say to ourselves and others, "I am committed to creating and sustaining mediocrity in everything I do and touch."

Quite the contrary!

In fact, each of our three major players in the conspiracy — leaders, HR and recruiters — has a clear commitment to deliver anything but average.

Whether leadership is thrust upon you, or whether you have long thought and dreamed about leading people, every leader has the same thought, whether or not it has even been articulated: "I can make a difference."

If you place this core statement in juxtaposition with the main areas of responsibility of most leaders, you can extrapolate a fascinating outgrowth of powerful beliefs that inform and influence all of a leader's actions.

- Leaders believe that if given the chance, they can positively impact others.
- They know that their actions can directly influence other's ability to be successful and achieve more. As a result, they can create an overall environment in which many people experience growth and success.
- They can articulate a compelling vision that others will grab onto and follow.
- They know they can either keep things organized and on track better than others — or they know they will surround themselves with people who are great organizers, leaving them the job of continuing to powerfully point the way for the organization to move forward.

No matter their background or the kind of organization to which they belong, every leader believes that their leadership will better equip their organization to deliver its promise more powerfully and more effectively to its intended audience. In fact, the commitment to make a difference extends beyond the people who comprise the organization to the people who the organization is serving.

Quite often, the individuals who assume and maintain positions of leadership are the highest-compensated people in their organizations. However, in my experience the desire to earn the highest levels of compensation is not the *raison d'etre* for why people become leaders. Compensation certainly plays a role in a leader choosing what organization he/she will join, but the drive to lead an organization has little to do with compensation.

No, the core statement for a leader can be simply stated:

Leader = I can make a difference.

Over my career, I have worked within the world of Human Resources and spent countless hours with various HR leaders, from managers to the most senior CHROs. Every individual who moves into HR has the desire and commitment to create and implement the various processes and overall infrastructure within an organization so that it can operate at the highest degrees of success, effectiveness and workability.

Think about the basic functional areas of human resources: compensation and benefits, hiring and staffing, policies around personal interactions with your co-workers, creating descriptions of different jobs, defining pathways of individual development and career progression, performance reviews, leadership assessment and development and more.

The commonality across each of these areas is not only "people." It is the actions and policies comprising the organizational infrastructure, that if running smoothly, maximize the organization's effectiveness and workability. If these actions and policies are not working well, the organization's effectiveness grinds to a halt.

Strategic HR is when the implementation of these processes, policies and actions directly impact the strategic goals and objectives of an organization. Each leader within an organization has a set of strategic goals and objectives, whether it is for the entire organization or for their functional or business component. A strategic relationship between a leader and HR exists when HR designs policies, takes actions and implements an infrastructure that make it easier for a leader to realize his/her strategic goals and objectives, and the leader recognizes this.

The core statement for HR is:

HR = I make things work better.

Lastly, whether recruiting is in-house or outsourced, whether it is for the lowest entry-level position or for the highest executive ranks, the underlying commitment of any recruiter is to bring a great person into a great opportunity. If a leader's commitment is "I can make a difference", and HR's commitment is "I make things work better", the commitment underlying every recruiter is, "I know that he/she will make a difference to the organization" and "I know that the organization will make a difference to her/him."

The core statement for a recruiter is:

Recruiter = I know that the candidate will make a difference to the organization and the organization will make a difference to the candidate.

These three basic commitments are the ground on which the three legs of the strategic stool stand, allowing an organization to grow and achieve greatness. But somewhere along the trajectory of an organization's life and the interplay of these three major players, these basic commitments are undermined by circumstances and statements that lead to the perpetuation of a state of average.

Of course, it can be useful to examine what it is about the nature of human beings and our interactions that allows a fundamental and defining commitment to be undermined. However, for the purposes of understanding how to build and maintain an organization of greatness, it is enough to simply recognize *that* this happens — that these core commitments are undermined by something else and that this occurs over time.

Given that this state of average is already a reality for most organizations, the way to unravel it is to begin identifying the overlapping statements we say to ourselves and others that arise from our circumstances. Like the different strands of rope in a massive Gordian knot, these statements maintain and reinforce this continued state of mediocrity and average.

3. THE GORDIAN KNOT

Our supposition thus far is that there is an unconscious conspiracy to maintain a state of average that permeates nearly all organizations regardless of structure (public, private, for-profit, non-profit), industry, geography and language spoken. Leaders, HR and recruiters are the unwitting three major players in this conspiracy.

Our three major players did not begin their careers with an eye on achieving a state of average and calling it a day. Rather, at some point in their lives, each developed an extraordinary commitment that fueled their chosen career pathways. These pathways each deliver our players into varied personal and professional settings and circumstances spanning their families, friends, schools and places of employment.

Within these varied settings, as circumstances develop and unfold, statements are initially made to our players and ultimately repeated by them. These statements occur in the moment as inherently making common sense. They appear as firmly grounded data points that on the surface, seem to support each player's formative commitment. In reality, these statements have an undermining effect. Over time they cause the formative commitment of each to be diluted and subsumed.

For the leader, while there may be an overarching statement of "I can make a difference", over time it is slowly minimized by statements such as:

- "I must deliver ongoing profitability and growth."
- "People (the organization/company) can only withstand so much change."
- "Any investment must be tied to growth."
- "I need to let my direct reports do their jobs with minimal interference."
- "The most important thing is for me to focus on what grows my business."
- "I need to very carefully pick where I challenge my board, investors, and shareholders."
- "Meeting our short-term objectives takes absolute precedence."

For the HR executive, while there may be an overarching statement of "I make things work better", over time this commitment becomes subsumed by statements such as:

- "We're doing the best we can with the resources that we have."
- "We can only push our business leaders and the organization so far."
- "We can only bring a transformational agenda to the table if our CEO and business leadership are supportive of it."

- "We need to crawl before we can walk."
- "Our business leaders can only understand so much."

For the recruiter, while there may be an overarching statement of "I know that the candidate will make a difference to the organization and the organization will make a difference to the candidate", over time this commitment becomes minimized by statements such as:

- "I need to fill this assignment as quickly as possible."
- "All that matters is finding someone to do the job at hand."
- "I need to find someone who fits in, not someone who challenges what's there."
- "Finding someone my client likes is more important than finding someone my client needs."
- "Why bother doing a detailed analysis of a candidate if it really doesn't matter to my client?"

These statements, and others like them, become the genesis for informing leaders, HR and recruiters of what is important and unimportant, what should be paid attention to or not paid attention to, how one should think about what they are doing or not think about what they are doing — and ultimately, the actions one should take or not take to deliver maximum desired results.

I am not suggesting that there is something inherently wrong about any of these statements. For a leader, focusing on growth, profitability, strategically picking your fights with your board/investors all are reasonable paths of action. For HR, intelligently managing resources and knowing your audience are critical to getting things done. For recruiters, certainly completing assignments/placing candidates and giving your clients what they want is part and parcel of the job.

However, over time, these statements that appear so reasonable and grounded on their own unintentionally have the effect of diluting — to outright negating — the initial powerful commitment that inspired the individual leader, HR executive and recruiter. This limits the possibilities inherent in each individual's career pathway, diminishing the potential impact that each of our major players will realize over their careers. And it doesn't stop there. This limiting affect spreads unabated into their organizations with a far and wide impact.

One of the main characteristics of an organization where our major player's core commitments have been subsumed by these diminishing statements is that the three players rarely threaten or challenge one another.

Leaders do not request, require or demand that HR and/or recruiters deliver something to them outside of what they already know and expect to receive. This cuts across all processes and activities. HR is perceived by the leader as a non-strategic yet necessary function, described in terms of "keeping the trains running on time" and "keeping us out of legal trouble." Such statements represent essential elements of HR, but are not necessarily strategic or transformative.

Recruiters are expected to do their job of filling positions — finding people who can sit in the organizations' empty seats so that the organization can keep on doing what it does. It becomes a numbers game across all elements of the process. It is not an exercise delivering a deep qualitative analysis where the recruiter discovers what is essential to move the organization strategically forward. Nor does the recruiter search for the qualities that any one individual candidate may or may not have that would allow him/her to achieve this result.

When leaders interact with HR and recruiters from this diminished perspective, they mirror back this same level of diminished expectations. HR and recruiters assume that leaders are not interested in anything other than what has been communicated, and that their leaders have a limited capacity for anything else. They know that their job is to do their job. As a result, HR and recruiters have an ever-diminishing set of expectations that their leaders will ever ask them to deliver anything outside the norm, and so this rarely occurs. HR and recruiters do their jobs within a context of "things will never be different", and "this is just the way it is" and thus ensure that is the case.

Our three major players interact with each other around areas and issues of people, specifically hiring, firing, coaching, mentoring, succession planning, leadership assessment and development. These are essentially all of the functions and actions surrounding the development of competencies and capacities of people within an organization. Thus, collectively these limiting statements produce an organizational state and culture where not much is expected of anyone other than that they keep doing their jobs and keep things going as is.

The result is that leaders, HR and recruiters act in perfect harmony with each other to produce an organization that is non-challenging and non-threatening across all its dimensions. They unknowingly become the major players in The Conspiracy of Average and thus ensure the perpetuation of the status quo.

3. THE SOLUTION

Perhaps there is something about the condition of being a human being that makes it exceedingly difficult for us to realize even our deepest commitments, since these commitments over time become subsumed and replaced by statements that seem totally reasonable and grounded to us but end up being significant limiting factors. Then is it possible for an individual to move beyond this apparently inescapable vortex to become a Leader of Greatness? And if so, how?

Similarly, given that organizations are all comprised of and populated by people — particularly the three major players we've described — who unknowingly are in the situation described above, then is it possible to break out of this status quo condition and create an Organization of Greatness?

Like many apparently complex and intractable problems, there is a simple solution that nonetheless requires hard work. But before we can even begin to address this solution, it makes sense to distinguish what the term "greatness" means in this context of both individuals and organizations.

Greatness is the highest state to which an individual and/or organization can aspire.

By greatness, I do not mean sustained success, financial or via any other criteria by which an individual or organization could be evaluated that would broadly be considered to constitute success. Although leaders and organizations of greatness most always also experience sustained success, this is a by-product of greatness. It is a result that occurs along the way, rather than the end-game.

Sustained success, even though it is difficult to achieve, is representative of a lower state of being than greatness.

Greatness also does not necessarily occur when an individual or organization are taking actions that have the highest degree of functional excellence and, as a result, lead to a state of effectiveness. Leaders and organizations who exhibit characteristics of high effectiveness and functional excellence almost always also experience sustained success; however, the reverse is not true.

There are many examples of individuals and organizations who sustain success over some period of time, but who do not exhibit characteristics of high functional excellence and effectiveness.

While it is difficult to achieve sustained success, this is actually a lower state to achieve than high functional excellence and effectiveness. And while high functional excellence and effectiveness generally embody sustained success, they do not necessarily also embody greatness. Hence, while high functional excellence and effectiveness is a higher state than sustained success, it is also a lower state than greatness.

So, greatness is more than sustained success, high functional excellence and effectiveness — but when greatness is present, you also generally find sustained success and high functional excellence. Then, what is greatness?

At its simplest, greatness has the possibility of occurring when two fundamental criteria are met:

1. The experience of shared value and contribution is present.
2. This experience makes a tangible difference with the individuals involved, regardless of whether they are the originators or recipients of the experience.

When these two criteria are repeatedly and reliably present, whether for an individual or a team, greatness is created.

Each of us can look into our lives and see many times where this kind of experience has occurred. You may in fact be saying to yourself, "This doesn't seem that different from what I attempt to do every day", and for most of us, this is accurate. However, even though this is what we attempt to do, and sometimes succeed at doing, the circumstances in our lives and careers, e.g., The Conspiracy of Average and the Gordian Knot, diminish our ability to sustain and repeat this experience. Instead, we find that these experiences of shared value and contribution are peak moments that stand out for us in stark contrast to the status-quo.

Interestingly, when the experience of shared value and contribution is repeatedly sustained, the Gordian Knot of mediocrity and average begins to lose its power. The vortexes of dis-empowering statements that seem reasonable and make so much sense begin to give way. When this occurs, a funny thing happens with our three major players of leaders, HR executives and recruiters.

They seem to get back in touch with their core commitments of making a difference, creating and implementing systems and processes that make things work better, and finding people who thrive in their positions and move the strategic needle forward across the entire organization. Instead of being subsumed by the Gordian Knot of reasonableness, they begin thinking, speaking and acting in a manner far more representative of their core commitments.

Could it actually be this simple? Could creating the experience of shared value and contribution on a repeatable basis really be the heart of creating leaders and organizations of greatness?

Yes, it is this simple, but simplicity does not necessarily mean that it is easy.

The recipe for creating leaders and organizations of greatness is, at its core, rather simple — but putting it into effect on a repeatable and reliable basis requires analysis, diligence and continued action. Too often for most of us, we believe that because we have a commitment to the extraordinary, that is sufficient to produce the extraordinary. However, in reality our commitment to produce the experience of shared value and contribution becomes an afterthought instead of forethought.

We assume because we know what the experience of shared value and contribution looks and feels like and have produced it before; we will naturally produce it over and over again in the course of our daily interactions.

This is similar to a baseball player who gets a solid hit assuming that every at-bat will deliver a similar result. However, within the world of professional baseball it is considered extraordinary for a player to get a solid hit 30% or more of the time. The ability to consistently hit home runs is even rarer. Over their careers, the best hitters throughout the history of baseball are able to hit homeruns 5% to 7% of their total at-bats.

The hitters that are able to achieve career batting averages over 300 and hit over 500 home runs often are voted into the Baseball Hall of Fame. They are considered the best at what they do and are spoken of as being masters of their craft.

Over the past several years, the concept of mastery occurring at 10,000 hours that Malcolm Gladwell wrote about in his book *Outliers* has become a part of popular vernacular and culture. In other words, mastery, e.g., sustained success and high-functional excellence and effectiveness, requires analysis, hard work, careful diligence and repeatable and reliable practice over time.

Given the universality of sports, it is easy to understand the inherent principles of attaining mastery. The same principles can be applied to any area of human endeavor, whether it is the arts (music, dance, drama, writing, poetry, painting, sculpting, etc.), or the sciences and business.

In any sport or feat of athleticism, practice is required to sustain success and be highly effective and functionally excellent at what you do. Anyone who has tried to master a physical act such as throwing a baseball, swinging a bat/golf club/tennis racquet, running for track, jumping hurdles, or executing the perfect butterfly stroke, knows that reliable and repeatable practice over time is essential. However, if all they are doing is practicing bad habits, a high level of effectiveness and excellence will never be attained.

In order to achieve mastery, they need to dissect and break down the elements of what at initial glance appears to be one fluid movement or action into smaller, separate steps. This allows the athlete, generally under the guidance of a coach, to isolate specific movements and make adjustments with the intention that the adjustments ultimately deliver a different and more powerful outcome.

Coaches work with athletes on recognizing these small steps, these specific movements, bringing discernment into the observation and analysis of their actions. Once the step or action is recognized, then minor adjustments can be introduced and the athlete can begin the process of practicing these adjusted movements and actions until they become part of who they are and how they approach what they do.

Each adjustment made often means training your body to develop new muscle memory. Over time and with enough practice, these separate steps are transformed into a natural easily flowing continuous swing, pitch, stroke or gait. They become a new and more powerful fluid movement.

This same process can be adapted to develop leaders and organizations of greatness.

In the context of developing leaders and organizations of greatness, the actionable event — the movement that is similar to a swing, pitch, stroke or gait — is the foundational structure of shared value and contribution. This structure can also be broken down into smaller separate steps, each with its own characteristics. If through careful discernment adjustments are noted and practiced, this ultimately results in reliably and repeatedly delivering the experience of shared value and contribution.

When the experience of shared value and contribution occurs on an ongoing basis, leaders and organizations of greatness are developed and brought forth. So like an athlete practicing these smaller steps, or a dancer practicing a particular set of moves, let us embark on distinguishing these smaller steps and characteristics that are contained within the one fluid movement that is the foundational structure for shared value and contribution — greatness.

5. IT STARTS AT THE TOP

At the highest level, the recipe for developing both leaders and organizations of greatness is to reliably and repeatedly create the experience of shared value and contribution. The key words "reliable and repeatable" in this statement point to a task that on its surface may seem easier to contemplate than actually produce.

Generally speaking, we know that the experience of shared value and contribution (referred to henceforth as "greatness") has occurred after the fact — often when a significant accomplishment has been achieved and, as the results become apparent, it becomes equally clear that something has happened that moved the accomplishment beyond the basic fulfilment of a goal or objective. Sometimes if we pay attention, we even have a feeling that something extraordinary is occurring or has the possibility of occurring while we are taking actions.

Even if we are cognizant enough of our surroundings, actions and the impact being experienced by those around us that we begin to realize that something extraordinary is taking place, we are naturally so engaged in our actions that we rarely stop and analyze what is happening that is giving us this inkling. Often in post-analysis of a significant set of tasks or accomplishments, we ask ourselves, "What made this project, this set of tasks, different?"

Typically we focus on the specifics of our actions. Rarely do we pay attention to the structure in which these actions took place. We don't think about and explore that there may be a larger context at work — a structure within which our actions and the actions of those with whom we participated fits. And yet that may be a significant contributor to creating this experience of "greatness."

If a structure of this nature could be distinguished, then logically an individual should be able to use this framework as a guide to stack the deck, if you will. We could make certain that the elements of this structure are in place, that individual actions are taken that are shaped to fit within this framework — and, in doing so, increase the likelihood that the experience of "greatness" results.

So the initial important questions are: Does a structure of this nature exist? Can it be distinguished? And if so, what does it look like?

There are two basic categories to the structure or framework of the experience of "greatness." One is contextual, the other action-oriented. Think of it as a meta-structure and a smaller action-oriented structure contained within the meta-structure. Both are deceptively simple.

Meta-Structure & Elements
- Powerful Personal and Inclusive Vision
- Shared Values
- Shared Strategic Goals
- Shared Accountability for Yourself and Team
- Representative Behavior/Actions

Whenever the experience of "greatness" occurs, these structural elements are in place. They are there regardless if they have been distinguished or not, or regardless of the degree of awareness existing about them.

If you look carefully at when you have been working with others and the experience of "greatness" occurred, you will find that there was always someone who had a powerful and inclusive vision that was in operation. There is always the sense that there are shared values that are guiding the actions taking place. There is always the awareness, even if it is nascent, that these actions are intended — and hopefully even designed rather than occurring by accident — to deliver something strategically important.

There is always a high degree of accountability that cuts across both individuals and the team around the actions that are being taken and their intended results. This shared accountability implies a level of accountability greater than an individual being accountable for his/her actions. Shared accountability means that not only are individuals personally holding themselves accountable, they are holding each other accountable across a group.

Lastly and most importantly, with respect to these actions, there are specific qualities or characteristics that are discernable even in the heat of the moment.

Think of it this way.

If someone was taking a video of the actions/interactions of an individual and team over the timespan that the experience of "greatness" occurred, would they see specific actions to which they could point? Actions that, from an observer's perspective, had discernable characteristics such that they could definitively say, "these were significant contributing factors to causing the experience of "greatness"? Also, if they took a video of a different occurrence containing different circumstances with a different group of people; would they see similar types of actions that had similar characteristics?

These discernable and repeatable qualities or characteristics of the actions taken when the experience of greatness occurs are the action-oriented structure contained within the meta-structure of "greatness."

In fact, you could say that the action-oriented structure is at the heart of the meta-structure, and hence at the heart of the experience of "greatness."

Action–Oriented Structure & Elements

The elements or characteristics of the action-oriented structure at the heart of the experience of "greatness" could be described, at a high level, simply as actions that are representative of the meta-structure. In other words, to go back to our analogy of the video, the actions being taken are so clear and strong that anyone watching the video should be able to infer and distinguish specific characteristics. They should be able to:

1. Clearly see that the actions being taken are representative of the highest expression of functional excellence and be able to specifically describe the representative actions.
2. Describe the intended strategic outcome of the actions.
3. Talk about the underlying vision that the strategic outcome is intended to deliver, e.g., not necessarily describe the exact wording of a well-thought-out and articulated vision, but certainly be able to infer and describe the overall direction and intent of that vision.
4. Describe the values that they believe are also underlying and informing the actions, and point to specific actions that are representative of these values.

These are the behavioral characteristics that comprise the elements of the action-oriented structure at the core of the experience of "greatness," and they are discernible every time the experience of "greatness" occurs.

However, if this meta-structure and action-oriented structure are the framework for delivering the experience of "greatness," and the reliable and repeatable generation of this experience is at the core of what constitutes both a leader and organization of greatness, can any individual, regardless of his/her hierarchical position or responsibilities in an organization, become a Leader of Greatness and through this create an Organization of Greatness?

Yes and no.

Clearly, any individual in any organization, no matter their role, responsibilities, hierarchical position or whether or not they are accountable for the actions of others in addition to themselves, can use this framework to reliably and repeatedly create the experience of "greatness".

By putting in place the meta-structure and action-oriented structure of "greatness," one person can certainly alter their own experience of what they do on a day-to-day basis. In doing so, they will make a tangible difference in the lives and work experience of those with whom they interact, not to mention making a difference in the level of value and contribution delivered to the individuals to whom their actions are directed.

However, the ability of an individual to leverage this experience to the broader organization, thereby increasing the probability that multiple teams begin working together to deliver an Organization of Greatness, is highly dependent on his/her hierarchical position within the organization.

No matter how successful an individual is in creating the experience of "greatness," on their own and within the circle of individuals with whom they interact the most, at a certain point — unless the senior-most levels of an organization adopt similar behavioral practices — an Organization of Greatness will not develop.

Even if you are a CEO, creating an Organization of Greatness is no small feat. Even if you adopt the meta-framework and action-oriented structure described, every CEO is confronted with the decision of what initiatives to champion, what processes become black and white, what are the defining characteristics that form the shape, color and experience of "being on the bus" — that if you do not ascribe to as an employee, you end up getting off the bus.

This is where for a CEO, not only does the rubber meet the road in terms of defining the kind of organization being built, it is also where the divergent forces at the heart of the Conspiracy of Average insert and reassert themselves.

The normal compromises a CEO makes to his/her deep-seated principles in the course of building and growing a company end up becoming the threads and substance of the Gordian Knot that keep the Conspiracy of Average in place. They become the gating factors that produce an organization that at its best is effective and successful, but certainly not one that achieves "greatness."

The building of an Organization of Greatness is deceptively simple, yet requires ongoing discipline, commitment and hard decisions. The meta and action-oriented structures outlined form a framework that a leader can leverage and fall back on, using the framework to define what it means to "be on the bus." This will lead to the development of a new kind of partnership with HR executives and recruiters — one that leverages the meta- and action-oriented structures, transforming the relationship between the unwitting co-conspirators in the Conspiracy of Average.

This transformation creates a partnership where leaders, HR executives and recruiters are all intentionally and consciously working toward creating an organization where the experience of sharing and delivering value and contribution becomes the new status quo.

6. BECOMING A LEADER OF GREATNESS

Organizations of Greatness do not happen by accident. They are created, nurtured and sustained by individuals who are committed to not only achieving sustained success and the highest levels of personal and organizational effectiveness, but who also take on the extraordinary commitment to create the experience of shared value and contribution in their own and their team's actions. Someone who does this is a Leader of Greatness. Becoming a Leader of Greatness is the necessary first step to building an Organization of Greatness.

We've distinguished both the meta- and action-oriented structures that underlie "greatness" (the experience of shared value and contribution). Our fundamental definition of "greatness" implies that that this experience is created through interactions with others. While this is true, there are a number of personal steps an individual can take that help attune and develop certain attributes, sensitivities, awarenesses and ultimately behavior that, when in place, pave the way for the easiest and most successful implementation of these structures that support "greatness" within a team and/or organization.

Just like building a house, these steps represent critical foundational bricks on which the framework of the house, i.e., the meta- and action-oriented structures, can be placed to ensure the integrity of the construction and its ability to withstand the pressures and vagaries of time and the environment.

The individual steps, or bricks in this foundation, are:

1. Articulating a powerful personal vision.

One of the fundamental steps of leadership on which all students of leadership behavior agree is the necessity to create and articulate a strong and compelling vision. However, even though this has been said by many authors and thinkers on leadership using different terminologies and in many different contexts, in practice many leaders and their organizations are confused about what this means.

With many leaders, their organizations and the consultants often hired to work with them, there is a blurring of the fundamental distinctions between what constitutes a vision versus a mission. Given the poor understanding of these distinctions, many so-called vision statements read instead like a set of marching orders describing short-term goals with specific steps listed to attain them — as opposed to a statement describing an aspirational future that nonetheless is grounded in present reality and creates the possibility of myriad pathways for action by individuals to fulfill this future state.

Additionally, quite often leaders bypass the step of devising and articulating a personal vision of leadership that has similar characteristics to what is listed above, and move right into attempting this exercise at an organizational level. Even if this results in a well-thought-out mission statement describing goals, objectives and the pathway for their realization as opposed to a vision, the execution and implementation of this often wrongly-characterized organizational vision will be limited by the fact that the leader has not developed a personal, aspirational vision that calls forth the highest level of thought and behavior on the part of the leader.

This does not mean that the sought-after results described in a mission statement of this nature cannot occur. It does mean that that the leader and organization's probability of achieving "greatness" will be significantly reduced. In fact, even if there truly is an organizational vision as opposed to a mission statement, if the leader does not take the time to develop a personal vision of leadership that is aspirational, the chances of creating and delivering an experience of "greatness" will be minimized. As we have already demonstrated, regardless of our best intentions, it takes an overarching commitment to overcome the Gordian Knot of circumstances and history and elevate oneself and an organization above The Conspiracy of Average.

While there can be many ways of articulating a powerful personal vision, the basic criteria in a successful personal vision statement is:

- It is future-based, describing a state that is not yet fully in existence but is nonetheless grounded in the present, and it is written in first-person singular present tense.

In contrast, a mission points to the present. It articulates the direction of the path to be walked and actions to be taken that will begin to fulfil on the future aspirational state described in the vision.

The words that you think and say about yourself and others are powerful tools to carve out and create the reality that you live into. Talking about yourself in a future-based vision statement using words and phrases such as "I will do" and "I will become" ensures that the forward-looking and aspirational qualities distinguished in your statement will remain qualities that are as yet-to-be and perhaps never realized.

When you use words and phrases in your personal vision statement similar to "I am" and "I have", you contextualize the sought-after behaviors in the present. You begin to think and speak of yourself as a leader who represents these qualities now, as opposed to thinking of yourself as a leader who may or may not someday realize your distinguished aspirational qualities.

While your personal vision speaks to a future aspirational state, it also needs to resonate with you, and with others, as having a basis of reality in the present. In other words, while your personal vision statement will articulate qualities, characteristics and results that you aspire to realizing in the future, (all in first-person singular present tense), you need to be able to viscerally get that this is not an ivory tower statement. You need to experience that even though your statement is painting an aspirational and future reality, you perceive that this reality has its roots firmly in the present.

- The personal vision statement is congruous with your self-leadership and ideal leadership definitions.

How would you define the qualities of leadership that are present in an ideal leader? How would you define the qualities of leadership that you would have if you and others thought of yourself as an ideal leader?

Your personal vision statement of leadership should distinguish these qualities and characteristics, and again articulate them in first-person singular and present tense.

- Lastly, your personal vision statement of leadership must be aligned with your values.

This does beg a series of questions. What are your values? How are they defined and described? How would you, or anyone, actually know that they are more than words written down on a piece of paper and are evident and discernable in your actions and behavior?

The answers to these questions comprise the full next step in building our foundation of individual leadership. Suffice it to say at this point that inquiring into these questions and beginning to incorporate some of the answers into your personal vision statement of leadership is a necessary component of moving you toward being a Leader of Greatness.

2. Fully fleshing out your values.
Values are an inherently complex phenomenon experienced and

understood on multiple levels and that have unique characteristics. For example, if you take a moment and think about any value you would describe as being important to you, and then ask, "What does this value mean?" you quickly discover that values are best described by using other values.

The value integrity is described by using the words honesty, truthfulness, completeness, accountability, ethical behavior, fairness, reliability, etc. The value collaboration is given further definition and meaning by words such as teamwork, cooperation, communication, acknowledgement, coaching, etc.

All of these additional descriptors are themselves values. Dependent upon the context or circumstances, any of these sub-values or key elements could be interchanged with the primary value as a more appropriate description for the moment. This phenomenon is equally true for all values, not just integrity and collaboration. When you dig into one value, you discover others; values have a unique interrelationship and interchangeable nature.

But perhaps the most important characteristic of values pertaining to the topic of "greatness" is that the most compelling evidence that any value exists in an individual can only be gleaned through the observation of that individual's actions and behavior.

In the context of becoming a Leader of Greatness, this means that in order to fully flesh out your personal values, you must not only identify their key elements, you must also bring the meaning of these values into existence by demonstrating them in your actions and behavior.

3. Identifying your biggest strategic commitments.

The next brick in our foundation of becoming a Leader of Greatness can be described most simply as a narrowing of your actions. This occurs through identifying the biggest strategic commitments for you and your team. Diffusion of focus across too many objectives is confusing. Determining the most critical strategic objectives amongst myriad possibilities and focusing on their realization is an essential step to becoming a Leader of Greatness and building an Organization of Greatness.

4. Identifying circumstances and individuals.

With the most important strategic objectives clarified, the next brick in building our foundation is to distinguish the circumstances you will most likely find yourself in, and the individuals with whom you will most likely be interacting in the context of fulfilling these strategic objectives.

There is both a current and future focus to this. Quite often when engaging in this exercise, it becomes clear that there are many circumstances, activities and individuals with whom you engage that are not essential to the fulfillment of your most strategic objectives. The answer to this dilemma is simple.

Stop putting yourself in these circumstances. Either have your interactions with these individuals be about fulfilling the strategic objectives of you and your team, or stop interacting with these individuals!

5. Identifying Appropriate Actions/Behavior.

One of the final bricks in constructing our foundation is to look at the work you have just done around circumstances and people, and begin to identify the specific actions you could take, the conversations you could have and the behavior you could exhibit that would be most representative of your personal vision of leadership and your set of values.

Identify the skills or experience that, if present and brought to bear within these circumstances, could make a positive difference in the realization of your strategic goals. Determine if these distinguished skills/experiences are ones that you have presently. If not, can they be quickly developed, or do you need to add individuals who have them to your team?

This is perhaps the most critical step in constructing our foundation for it requires the greatest degree of original thinking.

Generally speaking, we do not roll out of bed in the morning thinking, "What are the actions I could take and the behavior I could exhibit today that would most represent my values and further my most important strategic goals and objectives?"

This foundational step demands that you now begin to think about and plan your life in this manner.

It may seem daunting at first, but if you approach this step in a logical and sequential fashion, it is far easier to accomplish than initially imagined. In my work with clients, I have found that a spreadsheet can be a great tool to help with this step and process, using a simple X/Y axis to distinguish columns representing the various elements, and the new conversations, behavior, skills and experience that will be brought into existence.

Whatever tools used, it is essential to write down the actions, behavior and conversations you intend to have within the circumstances you have distinguished. It is not enough to just think it through. Get it in black and white. This is important from several perspectives.

Writing it down will help you manage the complex construction of these new words, actions and behavior, ensuring that they represent everything you intend. It serves the essential function of beginning to bring something new into existence by making it more tangible. It also will provide you with a record of what you intend to accomplish. This will allow you to best manage the last foundational step.

6. Practice, Implementation, Measurement and Evaluation

The final foundational step of becoming a Leader of Greatness is to practice and implement what you have distinguished, measuring and analyzing your results, and adjusting as needed. Given that the foundation being built thus far is within the context of your strategic objectives, you have created an ideal testing ground to bring these new conversations, actions and behavior into existence. This will allow you to even more quickly measure and evaluate your results.

What is the level of effectiveness of your communications and/or actions? Were you able to move a critical relationship forward? Were you able to affect greater alignment and generate increased commitment from others? Where did your communications/actions fall short and what could be brought to bear with new conversations and/or actions? What new people have you identified that are critical to moving your objectives forward?

Answering these questions and modifying your actions accordingly to deliver different results becomes an ongoing process of self-discovery for a Leader of Greatness. A structure of this nature that is put in place, monitored for results, and adjusted based on analysis becomes the foundation for creating the experience of shared value and contribution across a team.

The individual who is able to put this foundation into place, and reliably and repeatedly track and monitor its progress, is beginning to walk clearly down the pathway to becoming a Leader of Greatness. The next steps down this pathway are to take the lessons learned on a personal level and apply them to build an Organization of Greatness.

7. BUILDING AN ORGANIZATION OF GREATNESS

Our journey began with The Conspiracy of Average where we discovered that there are endemic conditions existing across many organizations that ensure the perpetuation of a constant and uninspiring state of mediocrity. Pay No Attention to the Man Behind the Curtain clarified the three major players of executives, HR and recruiters, and their respective roles in maintaining this conspiracy. The Gordian Knot began to unmask the overlapping and interconnected conditions which keep this state of average in place and subsume the foundational commitments of our major players.

In The Solution, we distinguished the formula or anatomy of "greatness" (the experience of shared value and contribution) for both an individual and organization, and in It Starts at the Top, we outlined the meta- and action-oriented structures at the heart of this experience. Lastly, Becoming a Leader of Greatness detailed the foundational steps necessary for an individual to firmly begin walking down the pathway of greatness.

In order to build an Organization of Greatness, these same foundational steps need to be leveraged and applied.

As at a personal level, attention needs to be paid to the differences between the distinctions of vision and mission in order to construct a powerful organizational vision. This vision must present a future state that is nonetheless clearly grounded in present experience and perception.

The most powerful organizational visions are simple statements that contain between five and nine words; the rule of thumb is that the fewer words, the better. While it is far easier to write a complex multi-sentence organizational vision, taking the time to distill even a nine-word vision down further is well worth the effort.

The organization's core values also need to be distinguished and described in greater detail through the articulation of their key elements. This can take the form of individual words or values-statements that often better contextualize the values and key elements in the work of the organization.

There are many methods that can be deployed to distinguish an organization's values, all of them valid. Regardless of the methodology used, from surveys to image or word cards to analysis of cultural artifacts and more, the most important components of distinguishing a rich set of organizational values is to again operate with the dictum that less is more, and to have the process driven from and owned by the organization's senior leaders.

Let's say you have fully fleshed out an organization's values and key elements. Now, if the resulting values-set is truly going to be used as more than verbiage on posters around the office or a page in an employee manual, it is essential that a maximum of six core values comprise the set.

Given the natural inherent complexity of just one fully fleshed-out value, replete with the identification of its key elements, representative actions and behavior, it becomes an impossible task for any individual and organization to work with too large a values set.

Again, less is more. Distinguishing more than six core values guarantees that the value-set will have little impact on the culture, strategic results and day-to-day behavior and actions throughout the organization.

Distinguishing a values-set containing six or less fully-fleshed-out core values does not necessarily guarantee greater impact, but it does allow you to apply this values-set in specific ways that can make a difference across your organization, its culture, your employees and the results you achieve. It allows you to enter the playing field and play the game of building an Organization of Greatness unencumbered by restraints of unnecessary complexity.

Our next foundational step is similar to the one noted to develop a Leader of Greatness. An Organization of Greatness needs to narrow its focus to the most important and critical strategic goals and objectives. Outlined over a one-, three-, and five- year time frame, these focused strategic goals become the framework within which an organization and its employees will take action.

The process of narrowing the organization's strategic goals will most likely also illuminate the extent to which the organization is consumed with non-strategic activities. As on an individual level, the organization needs to develop discipline regarding stopping non-strategic activities.

The next foundational step was to bring your set of personal values to life by identifying the circumstances and individuals with whom you would interact, and then distinguish the most values-representational actions and behavior that could be brought to bear within those circumstances. The last step was to practice these newly distinguished actions and behaviors, evaluate the results and adjust where and when necessary.

Given that the circumstances and people identified are all within the context of the most critical strategic goals and objectives, identifying effective actions/behaviors — or the opposite and making necessary adjustments — naturally has the result of forwarding these strategic goals.

At an organizational level, these last steps of identifying circumstances, individuals, strategic goals and objectives, and the implementation, evaluation and adjustment of new actions and behaviors have an even deeper strategic impact.

When these final steps are extended to an organization, instead of distinguishing individual actions and behavior, the same principles and methodology are used to design new actions and behavior across all functional areas.

This requires a new level of partnership and communication between the three major players distinguished in our Conspiracy of Average; e.g., leaders, HR executives and recruiters. When our three major players are acting together in this manner, a rich data set is created that can be used for multiple purposes across the organization.

This data set is developed by asking and answering the following questions for each functional area:

- With clarification of the most critical short- and long-term strategic goals for the organization, what is the relationship of each functional area to the accomplishment of these goals and what are the specific strategic goals that can be distinguished for each area over the next 12, 24 and 36 months?

- What are the circumstances that each functional area will most likely find themselves in over the next 12, 24 and 36 months as actions are taken to achieve these strategic goals?

- Who are the individuals, or groups of individuals (other teams) with whom each functional area will need to interact to fulfill these strategic goals?

- Given the skills and experience required for each functional area and the set of fully-fleshed-out values that have been distinguished, what are the actions that could be taken within these circumstances that leverage the required skills and experience to the greatest degree and have the highest representation of the values-set?

The rich set of data created for each functional area by leaders, HR and recruiters engaging with these questions can be used to develop:

- Holistic job descriptions that do more than list a generic set of required skills and experience. They instead:
    - Clearly articulate the most important strategic goals to be accomplished.
    - Identify the individuals and teams to be interacted with that are essential to the accomplishment of these goals.
    - Distinguish the actions to be taken that will realize these goals, and the skills, experience and the sought-after values representative behavior embedded within these actions.
- Interview guides that identify the values-representative and strategic behavior that can be used as the basis for the evaluation and assessment of all potential new hires.
- Performance appraisal criteria, that can be used as the basis for annual reviews, that identifies the sought-after actions to be taken and behavior to be exhibited that:
    - Contains the highest levels of required skills and experience.
    - Represents the organization's value-set.
    - Delivers on desired strategic goals and objectives.

If leaders, HR and recruiters partner with each other to create job descriptions, interview guides and performance appraisal criteria of this nature, they will be taking ownership of processes that all too often end up being one-dimensional rote exercises for most organizations.

How many job descriptions look the same from one organization to the next and are mainly a minimal list of required skills and experience? How many interviews occur across organizations that deliver very little knowledge beyond what can be gleaned from a resume review, and certainly give the interviewer no data that makes a difference in assessing the candidate's fit with the organization's culture and his/her ability to impact strategic goals and objectives? How many performance appraisals, if they happen at all, are exercises in checking boxes to satisfy HR requirements?

How many leaders and their teams go through these exercises with little conscious awareness of their importance and impact on developing leaders of Greatness and building an Organization of

Greatness?

In fact, if executives, HR and recruiters make a concerted effort to think through the questions posed above, the resulting job descriptions, interview guides and performance appraisal criteria naturally encompasses all the areas contained in both the meta- and action-oriented structures distinguished at the heart of the experience of "greatness."

Here again are both structures.

Meta-Structure of Greatness
1. Powerful Personal and Inclusive Vision
2. Shared Values
3. Shared Strategic Goals
4. Shared Accountability for Yourself and Team
5. Representative Behavior/Actions

Action-Oriented Structure of Greatness
1. Clearly see that the actions being taken are representative of the highest expression of functional excellence and be able to specifically describe the actions that were at this high level of excellence.
2. Describe the intended strategic outcome of the actions.
3. Talk about the underlying vision that the strategic outcome is intended to deliver, e.g., not necessarily describe the exact wording of a well-thought-out and articulated vision but certainly be able to infer and describe the overall direction and intent of that vision.
4. Describe the values that they believe are also underlying and informing the actions and point to specific actions representative of these values.

If leaders, HR and recruiters partner with each other in the manner outlined, they would be actively engaged in creating job descriptions, interview guides and performance appraisal criteria that represent clear frameworks for each functional area to deliver "greatness" across their organization.

This would deliver a significant blow to the Gordian Knot of conditions that keep the Conspiracy of Average in place!

When leaders, HR and recruiters are actively engaged in these processes, something magical occurs. Every interview, performance appraisal, and the discussions occurring post-interviews and performance appraisals, reinforce the actions and behavior necessary to bring the organization's values into greater existence and deliver sought-after strategic objectives.

Every candidate interview, performance appraisal, and even the act of creating job descriptions, becomes an exercise in leadership development. Finalist candidates hired will have a much higher probability of driving the organization to attain its aspirational culture. These candidates *will* become the desired and envisioned players that impact the organization. They *will* drive the achievement of strategic results.

Every performance review underscores the importance of bringing the organization's value set into on-the-job actions and behavior. This realization occurs for both the appraiser and employee being reviewed. The impact of all of these activities rolls out into the organization like the concentric circles from a pebble dropped into a pool of water.

Ultimately, when an organization applies these principles and tools in this manner, a culture of leadership occurs in which the experience of shared value and contribution is continually and systematically reinforced into the everyday actions and behavior across all functional areas and hierarchies.

An organization that does this has a much greater probability of achieving its strategic objectives and sustaining that success over time. It has a greater likelihood that in every nook and cranny of their organization, people will be acting with the highest levels of functional excellence and effectiveness and creating the experience of "greatness."

An organization that adopts and commits itself to this course of action will naturally hire, nurture and develop employees across all levels who become Leaders of Greatness and who together create and sustain an Organization of Greatness.

ABOUT THE AUTHOR

Greg Selker has been in the retained executive search and leadership consulting business for over 26 years. A former partner at one of the leading multinational executive search firms, he started his own firm in 2002 to create a qualitatively different approach that delivers value to both clients and candidates in what has become an increasingly transaction-based industry and marketplace.

Throughout his career, technology companies have been his focus, including those dealing in software, hardware, services and infrastructure, ranging from venture-backed start-ups to private-equity-owned mid-tier companies, to global multinational companies where he has worked extensively at both the board and executive management levels. He has also taken his knowledge of technology and particularly infrastructure to work with IT organizations and CIOs across multiple industry sectors.

Greg has personally completed hundreds of executive searches in his career, including many CEO searches. He has conducted Leadership Development Sessions with more than 50 executives from leading technology, pharmaceutical, professional services and manufacturing companies, moving into executive coaching relationships with numerous CEOs, CIOs, and CFOs.

He has co-led trainings given to hundreds of personnel on best-hiring practices and values-based interviewing across the senior leadership teams of many of these same companies, working personally in developing the leadership capacities and potentials of CEOs, CIO', CFOs and their senior leadership teams.

He is committed to a world in which every person is fulfilled and enlivened by what they do. His current executive search and leadership consulting activities are focused on realizing this commitment and assisting his clients to both become Leaders of Greatness and build Organizations of Greatness.

www.ingramcontent.com/pod-product-compliance
Lightning Source LLC
Chambersburg PA
CBHW051637050426
42443CB00025B/451